Archaeological Inventory
of the California Desert:
A Proposed Methodology

by

Margaret L. Weide
Archaeological Research Unit
University of California
Riverside, CA 92502

Prepared For The:

USDI – BLM
Desert Planning Program
1695 Spruce Street
Riverside, CA 92507

Order No. 04960-PH3-15

December, 1973

TABLE OF CONTENTS

INTRODUCTION

The California Desert includes a considerable quantity of archaeological resources along with its many other values. As the Bureau of Land Management seeks to meet the challenge of managing its desert lands for the common good, it is appropriate that the archaeology of the area be numbered among its considerations. Not only does the BLM have a legal responsibility to protect archaeological remains under Federal law, but archaeology constitutes a public resource in several respects. Understanding and enjoyment of the desert as a recreational area is enhanced by understanding the ways prehistoric man lived in this environment that strikes many as harsh and sterile. Archaeology is the raw material for the unwritten history of several of the California Indian peoples and is of special concern to them. It is also a scientific resource, a proving ground where archaeologists can test and revise their ideas about how man's long years as a hunter and gatherer shaped his modern lifeways, and through what socio-economic arrangements and technological developments man adapted to a wide variety of environments.

Basic to management is inventory, and inventory of archaeological resources on the scale of the California Desert is not easily accomplished. Proposed here is a sampling design to discover the patterns of location of archaeological resources in the desert and to make these patterns and projections derived from them available as a data base for management planning.

NEED FOR MANAGEMENT OF THE ARCHAEOLOGICAL

RESOURCES OF THE CALIFORNIA DESERT:

OUTLINES OF AN ARCHAEOLOGICAL PROGRAM DESIGN

The Bureau of Land Management has had the responsibility for protecting the archaeological resources of its lands under the U. S. Antiquities Act of 1906. These responsibilities have been spelled out and expanded by the Historic Sites Act of 1935, the Historic Preservation Act of 1966, the National Environmental Policy Act of 1969 and the Bureau of Land Management Manual sections 6231, 9351, 3509 and 3605. Federal lands such as those the BLM holds in the southern California desert, protected by the Antiquities Act and removed from centers of population concentration, constitute the major reservoir of undisturbed archaeological materials in the United States. These too are threatened. Current projections suggest that at the present rate of site destruction only 20-50 years remain before essentially all the archaeological remains in the country will have been destroyed. In less than 300 years man will have destroyed the evidence of more than 15,000 years of prehistoric occupation.

If the archaeology of the California Desert is not to slip away in the near future, a comprehensive program of preservation and management is required. Through lack of means of enforcement, the Antiquities Act of itself has provided little real protection. The resources that remain in the California Desert are there largely because of the lack of development and the relative inaccessibility of its remote areas, two factors that are rapidly changing as a result of increasing population in adjacent areas and greater mobility of that population.

The archaeological inventory of the California Desert is designed to provide inventory data on the nature, estimated numbers and distribution of archaeological resources in the desert. It is the basic step in developing an archaeological program design for the California Desert, which would include the following:

1. Inventory the archaeological remains of the California Desert;

2. Long term protection of archaeological resources from:

    a. Destruction by construction of facilities for increased use of the desert, and related impacts,

    b. Non-scientific exploitation including casual collecting, systematic collecting for sale, exchange or private use as decorations, etc.

    c. Damage by indirect effects of increased use of desert areas resulting in erosion and other disturbance of the surface;

3. An interpretive program to enhance public enjoyment of the desert through the opportunity to learn how earlier peoples used and viewed these same lands;

4. A program of public education that will result in the recognition of archaeological resources, along with other desert values, as fragile and easily destroyed, to be protected and conserved in the course of use of the desert;

5. Monitoring the scientific use of archaeological resources through existing and expanded federal policies requiring permits, justification of proposed work and reporting of results;

6. Enforcement of laws and policies relating to protection and proper use of archaeological resources;

7. Management planning to minimize direct and indirect impacts on archaeological resources;

8. Adequately funded program of archaeological survey and salvage permitting thorough recovery of archaeological information from localities where overall management considerations dictate that archaeological resources cannot be preserved;

9. Protection of lands reverting to BLM ownership until they can be inventoried for archaeological resources, recognizing that lands previously closed to public access, such as military reservations, may constitute unique preserves of relatively undamaged archaeological resources; and

10. Inventory of lands to be exchanged out of BLM ownership to assure that significant archaeological resources are not lost to public ownership and protection through such exchange.

OBJECTIVES OF THE ARCHAEOLOGICAL INVENTORY
OF THE CALIFORNIA DESERT

1. The discovery and recognition of patterns of ethnographic and prehistoric use of the Caifornia Desert area;

2. Identification of the biotic, topographic or hydrologic variables, or combinations thereof that form the most accurate predictors of archaeological locations;

3. Investigation of how well the variables employed in the Desert Study will predict the location of archaeological resources;

4. Development of projections of expected density and distribution of archaeological resources in the California Desert;

5. Delineation of areas of high archaeological sensitivity requiring maximum protection;

6. Delineation of areas with a high probability of lower archaeological sensitivity where development for economic or recreational activities should endanger relatively few archaeological resources, resulting in minimal costs for protection and/or salvage of what resources are present.

ASSUMPTIONS AND APPROACH OF THE

ARCHAEOLOGICAL INVENTORY

In approaching the problem of inventory by way of discovery of patterns of site location relative to a series of environmental variables and the development of projections based on these patterns, the archaeological inventory assumes that:

1. Extraction of economic resources was a significant determinant of the land use patterns practiced by the aboriginal inhabitants of the California Desert. Location of archaeological sites, therefore, will have a regular relation to the distribution of economic resources used by the past inhabitants;

2. While we do not know these past economic systems in detail, or how the distribution of economic resources has changed through time, we may expect that they are closely related to current plant zones, physiography and hydrology; and

3. That relations between these variables and archaeological locales are of sufficient strength that predictions of site densities and locations can be generated for management purposes.

The first assumption is well justified in anthropological theory, although how _much_ of site location can be accounted for by the distribution of economic resources remains under study. It is expected that this factor will vary through time, between cultural groups and with different levels of socio-economic organization. With respect to the second and third assumptions, similar work underway in restricted areas of the desert, Great Basin and

American Southwest indicate these are reasonable assumptions. From the viewpoint of archaeological theory, the archaeological inventory of the California Desert constitutes a large scale test of these assumptions.

KINDS OF DATA NECESSARY

Non-Archaeological Data

The archaeological inventory requires a non-archaeological data at two junctures, first in stratifying the inventory area prior to drawing the samples, and later, in the analysis of site locations.

Three prime variables, hydrology, vegetation and physiography, will stratify the random sample of areas to be examined, assuring large scale projections of site densities for the inventory area. For each of these variables the archaeological inventory will require maps of the inventory area divided into zones according to these three variables. Table 1 shows the magnitude of the subdivisions of the stratifying variables. Generally they should correspond with or be closely related to the first-order sub-divisions of the Legend of the pertinent BLM Inventory, as worked out for Vegetation, the only legend available at present.

In analyzing the locations of occupation sites and camps, the archaeological inventory will require non-archaeological data from a wider variety of disciplines and at a more detailed scale. Site catchment analysis, a prime tool in identifying patterns of site location, focuses on the amounts and varieities of economic resources available within a given range of a site. In dealing with peoples lacking vehicles and domesticated transportation animals, the radius of the area of analysis is an estimate of the distance which someone can walk, accomplish economic tasks and return within a day. It is usually estimated at 5-10 km from the site. Within this radius the following kinds of data are pertinent to hunting and collecting peoples.

a. Vegetation: density and distribution of plant species, especially those of economic values;

TABLE 1 - STRATIFYING VARIABLES

A. Vegetation[1]

Archaeological Inventory Stratum	BLM Vegetation Map Legend Communities	BLM Code
A_1	Saltbush Communities	13
	Creosote Bush Communities	11
A_2	Desert Shrub Communities	16
A_3	Mountain Shrub Communities	05
	Conifer Communities	06
	Pinyon-Juniper	09
A_4	Grass Community	01
	Sagebrush Community	04

B. Hydrology[2]

B_1 Springs and tanks, area defined as a circle .5 km radium from the spring or tank.

B_2 Stream order less than three, area defined as a strip 1 km wide centering on the stream line.

B_3 Stream order three or larger, area defined as a strip 1 km wide centering on the stream line.

B_4 Areas within .5 km of relict features of past hydrology, such as past lake stands, now-dry washes, springs and tanks.

B_5 Areas at distances greater than .5 km from water resources as defined above.

C. Physiography[3]

C_1 Sand dunes.

C_2 Basin floors and valley floodplains.

C_3 Bajada slopes and alluvial fans.

C_4 Mountain/bajada intersection, area defined as a strip 1 km wide centering on the break in slope.

TABLE 1 - continued

$C_5{}^4$ Slopes with exposed bedrock and/or greater than 10% slope.

C_6 Upland surfaces with less than 10% slopes.

Notes:

[1] Strata defined under Vegetation can be mapped directly from completed BLM Vegetation maps for the Desert.

[2] At the time of this writing it is not known what form water resources maps for the desert inventories will take. The subdivisions of this stratifying variable should be considered subject to adjustment to better utilize water resource inventory data when it becomes available.

[3] It is not now known how the BLM will handle physiographic classification. It appears that the physiographic classification implicit in the Soils Legend at the Soil Series level could be adapted to serve as a stratifier in the archaeological element if the BLM Inventory does not include a more explicit landform classification.

[4] In areas where local lithology favors the development of caves and shelters, outcrop areas can be defined as a substratum and examined in second phase sampling.

b. Soils map;

c. Current hydrology including flow estimates, reliability and long term parameters of flow variation;

d. Wildlife: density, distribution and seasonal patterns;

e. Lithologic resources, particularly the availability of cherts, obsidian and crystalline rocks for chipped stone manufacture;

f. Relict features of past hydrologic and pedologic regimes; and

g. Evidence of botanical and faunal changes, introduced species.

Ethnographic-Ethnohistoric Data

The record of desert land use in the period just preceding and subsequent to European contact constitutes the richest part of the desert's archaeological record, the time segment with the greatest potential for understanding and interpreting aboriginal use and occupancy in the desert. The archaeological resources dating to this period are complemented by the existence of written materials of ethnographic and ethnohistoric content. Only for this period do direct records exist of aboriginal life in the California Desert. Compilation of the ethnographic and ethnohistoric information is vital to meaningful interpretation of the late prehistoric archaeology of the desert, and constitutes a prime source for meaningful models to be tested against the archaeological record. Once compiled, this information will constitute a tremendous data base for BLM interpretive programs enhancing the public's understanding and appreciation of the California Desert.

Compilation of ethnohistoric data will emphasize:

1. Ethnobotanical survey to identify economic plants used by the several Indian groups of the desert, along with quantitative data as to their importance and role in the socio-economic life;

2. Ethnofaunal survey with similar goals;

3. Evidence of site locations from oral literature, ethnographic surveys and Spanish documents;

4. Survey of material culture collections and associated notes and data from museum files for evidence of site location, technology and economy; and

5. Survey of photographic collections for archaeological and ethnographically relevant pictures.

Three general kinds of resources exist for the ethnographic-ethnohistoric component; published materials, archival materials and Native Americans who combine their knowledge of present Native American cultures with research into written sources and can provide a most vital perspective. Ethnographers and ethnohistorians have recently located a wealth of published and archival materials bearing on the aboriginal inhabitants of the California Desert, scattered in a dozen or more institutions throughout the country. They must now be combed to retrieve the data useful to the archaeological inventory and as interpretive materials.

Direct benefits to the archaeological inventory include:

1. A complete map of ethnographically and historically documented sites and their classification by tribe and where possible by use, structures and features;

2. A thorough description of potential biotic resources available in each area from the ethnographic view;

3. Documentation of known trade and exchange relationships; and

4. A catalog of artifacts for which there is ethnographic data as to their culture of origin, techniques of manufacture and/or uses and functions for comparison with archaeological materials.

Archaeological Data

The archaeological inventory requires the identification and study of a representative sample of archaeological sites in each inventory area. The internal organization of the site must be recorded so that it can be categorized as to the kind of site it is. In addition, remains of tools and objects will have to be examined to determine the general time periods of its use.

Categorization of a site as a temporary camp, quarry, semi-permanent village, etc. requires data on the size of the site, presence of any structural remains, associated permanent features such as bedrock grinding surfaces or rock art, distribution of tools and refuse on the surface reflecting activities carried on at the site and a general summary of the artifact inventory present. Assignment of the site's occupation period(s) requires identification of temporally significant artifacts on its surface, which in the desert will be primarily projectile point types and pottery types. Specifics of archaeological data requirements and collection are spelled out in the section on Execution of the Sampling Design.

Remote Sensing

The activities of prehistoric man in the desert areas in many cases did not modify the surface of the earth sufficiently to be distinguished on aerial photography or ERTS imagery, so that remote sensing techniques will not record many of the loci of man's activities. Among those prehistoric features that can be discerned by remote sensing at appropriate scales are rock constructions such as ground figures and fish traps, mescal roasting pits, "sleeping circles" and trails in desert pavement, and irrigation channels.

While locations and distributions of the above kinds of archaeological sites can be studied directly on aerial photos, most occupation sites will not be visible on photos. In inventorying the bulk of desert sites, remote sensing will have a two-fold role. First, the large scale mapping of terrain with respect to the several variables of concern in archaeological locational analysis will make possible investigation of the distribution of archaeological resources at a scale not possible before. Results of archaeological locational analysis can then be extended to additional areas of the desert where natural resources mapping is available, greatly extending the results of the archaeological inventory. Second, availability of map correlated aerial photographs will enhance the speed and accuracy for the on-the-ground field work portion of the archaeological inventory. Used in conjunction with topographic maps they speed up location of quadrats to be examined, delineation of site limits and site-catchment radius to be examined, and provide rapid orientation to a site's microenvironment.

Once patterns of site location and site density relative to vegetation, hydrology and physiography have been established for the California Desert by studies in inventory areas, remote sensing can provide large scale mapping of these biotic variables, from which projections of expected site locations, densities and archaeologically sensitive areas can be made for the Desert as a whole.

BLM INVENTORY AREAS AS SAMPLING UNIVERSES

The Bureau of Land Management is approaching the California Desert through resource inventory of a series of inventory areas within the desert. These are being selected to represent the several subregions of the desert areas with consideration given to land ownership patterns and man's current impact on the desert. While the inventory areas selected by the BLM will not form a probability sample of the desert this limitation is more than offset by the advantages to be gained by coordinating the archaeological inventory with other inventories.

Present BLM plans call for large scale mapping of inventory areas with respect to soils, vegetation, water resources, minerals, geology and wildlife. By working with BLM inventory areas archaeologists will be able to draw on these detailed studies and maps to stratify inventory areas for sampling. In analysis phases, control of these variables will expedite microenvironmental analysis of site locations, permitting control of more variables at a finer level than were used to stratify the sample.

In the archaeological inventory, each inventory area will constitute a universe for sampling purposes. Consistent use of the sampling procedure outlined here in all inventory areas will produce a set of consistent data for each inventory area, from which statements about site locations in the desert as a whole and in the subregions can be made.

Prior to initiating the sampling strategy in any inventory area a thorough background study should be completed, summarizing the available knowledge of the area's ethnohistory, ethnography and prehistory, and assembling site records and locations for all recorded archaeological sites in the area.

GENERAL SAMPLING STRATEGY/TECHNIQUE

FOR ALL INVENTORY AREAS

Multistage stratified random sampling is judged the appropriate sampling design for the archaeological inventory of the Desert Study. As a form of random sampling it will yield a probability sample and will permit calculation of the reliability of site density estimates projected from these samples. Stratification of the random sample provides two basic guarantees; first, a fair allocation of the samples within the inventory area, and second, assurance that site density distribution estimates relative to the basic management variables selected as stratifiers will be forthcoming as central, basic results of the study. Two-stage sampling permits allocation of the samples in ways to maximize the information yield for a given amount of field time.

Archaeological judgment and the assumptions of the archaeological inventory direct that three major variables, vegetation, hydrology and terrain physiography, be selected as stratifying variables. Following Kish's admonition (1965:101) that "Generally, more gain accrues from the use of coarser divisions of several variables than from the finer subdivisions on one," the proposed divisions of the stratifying variables are outlined in Table 1.

Sample Size and Allocation

No rule has been established as to size of sample or sampling percentage necessary for a study such as this. Plog and Hill (1971:21) discussing the American Southwest state, "In order to analyze the effect of the variables independently and in interaction we will need to sample territory that falls within each of the extant sets... Somewhere between 25% and 50% of the territory covered by each set should be samples. Twenty-five percent seems

to be the sampling percentage necessary to obtain minimal accuracy while 50%
sample frequently seems necessary before really substantial accuracy can be
obtained." Several studies now underway in the Great Basin (Thomas 1969;
Bettinger 1973) are utilizing a 10% sample, with disproportionate allocation
of the sample between strata. These sample sizes have been determined
entirely by operational pragmatics. Thomas says "Since this is a pilot study
in every sense and we cannot therefore make even a reasonable estimate as to
the sample variance, we are in no position to calculate proper sample size;
the sample must be determined strictly on economic considerations (1969:92-93)."

Economic considerations rule out samples of the size suggested by Hill and
Plog. On the other hand, 10% samples such as those being used with some
success by Thomas and Bettinger in well watered valley systems in the Great
Basin may not yield an adequate number of site locations for analysis due to
lower expected site densities in the California desert. The sampling design
proposed here is a multistage stratified random sample, examining an area
equivalent to 15% of the land surface of the inventory area with disproportionate
allocation of that 15% among the strata. Tables 2a, 2b, 3a and 3b summarize
the expected results of such a sampling design in two hypothetical inventory
areas.

The first stage sample includes 5% of the land surface of the inventory
area, allocated proportionately to all strata. Field survey of the first-stage
quadrats will allow identification of zones of very low densities which can
then be dropped from further sampling, allocating remaining field time to
zones where larger numbers and/or particularly significant sites may be
expected.

TABLE 2a - MODEL STUDY AREA 1

Assume Inventory Area = 500,000 acres

   3/4 of area has low site density, averaging 1.5 sites per square mile,

   1/4 of area has high site density, averaging 6.0 sites per square mile,

   15% survey = 75,000 acres to be surveyed.

First Stage Sample:

   5% of all zones, 25,000 acres to be allocated proportionately.

      3/4 of 25,000 = 18,750 acres at low density, or 29.3 sq. mi. at low
      density - expected site sample = 29.3 x 1.5 = 43.95 sites

      1/4 of 25,000 = 6,250 acres at high density, or 9.77 sq. mi. at high
      density - expected site sample = 9.77 x 6 = 58.62 sites

   Total site sample expected, first stage: 43.95 + 58.62 = 102.57

Second Stage Sample:

   10% of all zones, 50,000 acres, to be allocated to high density areas,
   1/4 of study area or 125,000 acres

   $\dfrac{50,000}{125,000}$ = 40% of area in priority strata will be surveyed in second
   stage sample

   50,000 acres = 78.125 sq. miles @ 6 sites/sq. mi.

   Expected site sample, second phase = 468.75

TOTAL SITE SAMPLE EXPECTED, MODEL STUDY AREA 1 = 571.32 SITES

Note that this sampling design provides for survey of 56,250 acres of high
density lands, constituting a 45% sample of these lands, and constituting
a sampling comparable to that recommended by Plog and Hill for selected
strata within the sample.

TABLE 2b - EXPECTED DISTRIBUTION OF SITE SAMPLE

MODEL STUDY AREA 1

Assume:

1. Village or large occupation sites comprise 10% of the sample

2. The remaining 90% includes quarries, workshops, rock art, temporary camps, milling stations, etc.

3. All village sites are datable

4. 25% of other sites are datable

5. Sites decrease in geometric proportion to their age.

Expected Ratio:

Period		Dates	Ratio	% Equivalent
I.	Marana	1300-Historic	5	33
			8	
II.	Haiwee	600-1300 AD	3	20
III.	Newberry	1200 BC-600 AD	4	26.7
IV.	Little Lake	4000 BC-1200 BC	2	13.3
V.	Mojave	? -4000 BC	1	7

Total Sites = 571.32 (571)

  57 Village Sites
514 Other Sites, 25% (129) datable

Expected Distribution:

Time Period	Village Sites	Other (datable)
I	19	43
II	11	26
III	15	34
IV	8	17
V	4	9
TOTAL	57	129

TABLE 3a - MODEL STUDY AREA 2

<u>Assume Inventory Area = 500,000 acres</u>

1/10 of area has high density, averaging 6 sites per square mile,

9/10 of area has low density, averaging 1.5 sites per square mile,

15% survey = 75,000 acres to be surveyed.

<u>First Stage Sample:</u>

5% of all zones, 25,000 acres, to be allocated proportionately.

1/10 of 25,000 acres = 2,500 acres at high density, or 3.91 sq. mi. at high density - expected site sample = 3.91 x 6 = <u>23.4 sites</u>

9/10 of 25,000 acres = 22,500 acres at low density, or 35.16 sq. mi. at low density - expected site sample = 35.16 x 1.5 = <u>52.73 sites</u>

Total site sample expected, first stage: 23.4 + 52.73 = 76.13 sites

<u>Second Stage Sample:</u>

10% of all zones = 50,000 acres to be allocated to highest density areas equalling 1/3 of the area, including the 50,000 acres of high density and 117,000 acres which averages 2 sites/sq. mi. Assume proportionate allocation of sample within this third.

$\frac{50,000}{125,000}$ = 29.94% of higher density area to be surveyed

29.94% of 50,000 acres = 14,970 acres @ 6 sites/sq. mi.
14,970 acres = 23.4 sq. mi. x 6 sites = <u>140.34 sites</u>

29.94% of 117,000 acres = 35,029.8 acres @ 2 sites/sq. mi.
35,029 acres = 57.4 sq. mi. x 2 sites = <u>109.5 sites</u>

Total site sample expected, second stage: 140.34 + 109.5 = 249.84 sites

TOTAL SITES EXPECTED, MODEL STUDY AREA 2 = 73.13 + 249.84 = <u>325.97 SITES</u>

TABLE 3b – EXPECTED DISTRIBUTION OF SITE SAMPLE

MODEL STUDY AREA 2

Assume:

Same assumptions in Table 2b hold.

Total Sites = 325.97 = 326

  33 Village Sites
293 Other Sites, 25% datable (73)

Expected Distribution:

Time Period	Village Sites	Other (datable)
I	11	24
II	7	15
III	9	19
IV	4	10
V	2	5
TOTAL	33	73

The second stage sample is an area equivalent to 10% of the total study area, but allocated only to priority strata, strata selected for further sampling on the basis of the first stage sample. For example in model study area 1 (Table 2a), a 500,000 acre study area, the second stage sample of 10% will permit examination of 50,000 acres. As a result of the first stage survey, strata comprising 1/4 of the study area were determined to be priority strata. Thus in the second stage sample, strata comprising 125,000 acres are to be sampled, by quadrats which will total 50,000 acres. This examination of 50,000 acres of a total of 125,000 acres in the priority strata constitutes a 40% sample of those priority strata, falling within Plog and Hill's recommended 25-50%, but for the selected strata only. It is recommended that priority strata for second stage examination be defined so that they include no more than 40% of the original study area, assuring adequate sampling of these strata in the second stage.

EXECUTION OF THE SAMPLING DESIGN

USGS 15 minute series topographic maps are uniformly available for the California Desert area and will serve as the base map for the archaeological inventory. A mosaic of the 15 minute sheets for all quads in the inventory area should be prepared as the base for stratification. Using BLM inventory maps, the study area should first be subidivided into the prescribed vegetation zones. The vegetation zones should then be subdivided into physiographic areas. The final subdivision will then be by hydrology, identifying the zones with positive water resources. Each delineated area should then be identified by its strata. For instance, all areas marked A_2 B_2 C_4 would be included in the stratum of areas with Desert Shrub vegetation communities adjacent to low order streams at the mountain-bajada interface.

To draw the sample a rectangular grid of dots spaced at .5 km intervals, keyed to the Universal Transverse Mercator Grid on the base maps would be superimposed on the stratified map, each representing the center of a possible quadrat. Each dot in each stratum would be numbered starting with 0001. The number of quadrats constituting a 5% sample of each stratus is calculated. Using a four-digit random numbers table, the requisite number of quadrats are selected for each stratum and the selected quadrats are outlined on the base map. Note that the position of the center of each quadrat determines which strata it represents. If its boundaries transgress a stratum boundary, that fact is ignored for the purposes of drawing the sample.

In drawing the second phase sample each stratum is identified with the percentage sample to be drawn from it converted to the number of quadrats to be examined. Using the 4-digit random numbers table once again, the requisite

number of quadrats are drawn for each stratum and the selected quadrats
outlined on the base map.

Suggested Organization of an Archaeological Team

The basic field unit would be a team of six archaeologists with a chief.
A group this size can be transported in a single vehicle and can maintain
verbal communication while walking transects. Team members would work as
equivalents while walking transects but would have specific responsibilities
when recording a site. Intra-team site recording responsibilities would be
generally as follows:

1 individual	prepare field map of site area and its internal organization; person must be skilled in basic mapping/surveying techniques
1 individual	record chronologically significant artifacts by drawing and/or photography; person must be well acquainted with regional archaeology and chronology, and skilled in drawing and photography
2 individuals	reconnoiter the site, determining its extent on the surface, flagging features, chronologically and functionally significant artifacts for recording, assist in mapping by holding tapes, etc.
2 individuals	reconnoiter the area with 1/2 km radius of the site for vegetation, water sources, particularly covering any areas that were not covered within the quadrat; persons must be well acquainted with the basic economic plants used in the area, and be able to recognize lithic resources and evidence of relict hydrology
chief	coordinate recording of site, decide if sample of surface assemblage is required, lay out sampling tracts within site if needed.

Utilization of helicopter time to transport crews to and from quadrats
would result in a considerable increase in efficienty of field crews,
particularly in areas where road access is limited and/or long distances must
be covered in moving between quads and from base camps to quadrats.

Field Procedures

Field procedures begin with locating a corner of the quadrat with the aid
of compass, map and aerial photographs. Each quadrat should be covered by a
series of parallel transects spaced about 20 m apart, depending on terrain,
with the team chief maintaining line and distance by compass and pacing.
Thus a crew of six can cover a quadrat in four sweeps, each member walking 2 km.
Each team member is supplied with an abstract quadrat map. On observing an
artifact or evidence of occupation the team member stops, calls to members on
either side and they jointly determine if they have an isolated occurrence or
a site. If the former, it is identified and plotted on the quadrat diagram
and the transect continued. If it is determined to be a site, the locale is
called to the attention of the team chief and recorded or flagged for intensive
examination and recording at the completion of the survey quadrat.

Recording a Site

In recording a site, three categories of on-site data collection are
needed: a map, a record of the chronologically significant artifacts and a
record of structures, features, and activity areas evident on the surface.
The basic document is a map of the site, which in most cases can be prepared
with compass, tapes and a farmer's level, all of which are readily portable.
The map will record the surface extent of the site, all archaeological
features, the character of the surface topography and cover, and areas of
disturbance. Point locations of functionally and/or chronologically significant
artifacts will be recorded on the map, as will locations of exposures that
indicate depth of deposit. Concentrations of chipping waste, artifacts, etc.
will also be entered. If a sample of the surface assemblage is judged necessary,
sampling tracts will also be entered on the map.

All artifacts of potential chronological significance or diagnostic of major site activities will be drawn and photographed and left in place (see Collection Policy below). Off-site reconnaissance will examine a 1/2 km radius from the site, annotating vegetation maps for that area, identifying water resources and lithic resources such as quarries, lithology of local gravels, etc., and checking for adjacent activity loci such as petroglyphs.

Information collected for each site will provide the following comparable data when synthesized.

A. The Site - its location in the Universal Transverse Mercator System, and in longitude and latitude

   1. Kind of site
      a. permanent or semi-permanent base camp, judged by size, density and variety of artifacts present
      b. limited activity site
         (1) milling station without chipping detritus
         (2) milling station with small quantity of chipping detritus and/or sherds
         (3) chipping detritus or sherd scatter only, or a small quantity of both
         (4) occupied shelter or cave
         (5) petroglyph and/or pictograph
         (6) ground figure
         (7) quarry or quarry/workshop
         (8) roasting pit(s)

   2. Condition
      a. pristine
      b. eroded
      c. collected
      d. damaged by vandals, pothunting, or other activity
      e. excavated previously

   3. Size in area

   4. Evidence of depth deposit

   5. Structures, features, activity areas present

   6. Slope, and lithology of on-site features, internal topography, soils

   7. Dating, assignment to time period in Descal Series (Bettinger and Taylor 1973), see Table 2b

B. Its Microenvironment[1] - data from field observations will be combined with data from other elements of the Desert Study inventory, maps and aerial photography

    1. Water resources, distance from site, kind, estimated flow, reliability; relict features of past hydrology

    2. Major economic plants; presence/absence and densities of such plants as
        Pinus
        Quercus
        Prosopis, Acacia, Palo Verde, Ironwood
        Agave, Yucca
        Opuntia, Echinocactus
        Prunus

    3. Number and areas of plant communities within designated radii of the site

    4. Presence of lithic resources

    5. Game, availability, density, seasonality

Artifact Collection Policy

The archaeological inventory requires that information be gathered at each site which will identify its general chronological position and its general nature, to the extent that this is possible without excavation. As a rule this information is obtainable from careful observation and recording at the site. For this reason, no standard methods of surface collection are included in the procedures outlined. A number of circumstances may occur in the course of inventory work where samples of the surface assemblage are required. Included would be situations where an institution is carrying on research in conjunction with their inventory work, instances where laboratory study is needed to clarify chronological significance of artifacts, cases where

-----

[1]
    The area within 1/2 km of the site will receive immediate field study. Zones of 5 km and 10 km radius around village sites, complex midden sites, milling sites and caves or shelters containing complex midden should be examined by maps and aerial photographs for potential resources inventory. The designated radii, 5 km and 10 km are based on the known distances exploited by modern hunter-collecters (Jarman 1972:713).

lithic frequencies of detritus may provide important time-space controls, etc. Collection is not proscribed from the archaeological inventory, but should be undertaken only when the need is clearly articulated, and then the sampling technique adopted should be designated to suit those needs.

Handling of Incidentally Discovered Sites

In the course of work in an area, sites will be found in travel between quadrats, etc., which do not fall into the inventory sample. Such sites should be recorded in the same manner as sites found in quadrats. Information from these sites must be kept separately and not used in any analysis or estimating techniques dependent on probability samples.

PROGRAM OF EVALUATION AND SYNTHESIS

Data output of the archaeological field teams will be continually monitored, permitting on-line evaluation of the progress of the archaeological inventory. Monitoring will focus on three aspects of the work progress, using estimated projections as controls:

1. rate of quadrant examination;

2. rate of site discovery per quadrat; and

3. data quality, how many sites can be dated and assigned to kind on the basis of field examination.

Continual monitoring of the data output will provide for quick recognition of any problems that arise in operationalizing the archaeological inventory. This continuous monitoring in combination with the 2-phase sampling design, where allocation of the second stage will be determined at midstream in the study, should assure discovery of sufficient sites for a meaningful analysis and significant results.

Four foci will form the core of the data synthesis; areal site density estimates, relationship of management variables to site locations, examination of additional variables collected by the archaeological teams relative to site location, and site catchment analysis. Site density estimates will be calculated as direct blow-up estimates by areal zones corresponding to the strata in the sampling design and will provide areal overlays reflecting differing expected densities for the study area.

Second level analysis will identify the patterns of site location relative to the main variables of the archaeological inventory, the three stratifying variables of vegetation, hydrology and physiography. The actual distribution of sites in the sample relative to each variable can be compared with the expected distribution if the variable has no effect on distribution, to identify the variables that affect the actual distribution. The sample of sites from the inventory area as a whole will be examined relative to each variable. Next, subsets of the site sample will be examined to identify non-random distributions relative to the several variables. Prime subsets should be defined by time period and by kind of sites. Where sample size permits, site subsets defined by both time period and kind of site, such as semi-permanent sites of the Haiwee period, should be examined relative to each variable. Since this data consists of category frequencies, primiarly on a nominal scale, non-parametric statistics are appropriate, and Chi-square is an appropriate statistic to test for significance of the above distributions (Siegel, 1956). The distribution of the site populations and its subsets will also be examined relative to combinations of the stratifying variables. Plog and Hill (1971:28-31) suggest percentage point difference as a useful way of looking at this kind of data, and again Chi-square provides an appropriate test of significance. Comparison of the distribution of site subsets by similar statistical means will sharpen the definition of the patterns of site location appropriate to the several subsets.

The third level of analysis will focus on distribution of the site population and its subsets relative to variables beyond the stratifying variables such as lithology, soils, specifics of on-site vegetation; also on additional variables defined pertinent to the specifics of the particular inventory area in question. For instance, in the limited areas of the desert where prehistoric agriculture may have been practiced, special variables pertinent to agricultural patterns should be defined and studied in addition to the core variables outlined here.

At the fourth level the analysis shifts from the site itself to examination of the microenvironment selected for a site location. The area around the site, defined by 5 km and 10 km radii and called the site catchment (Vita-Finzi and Higgs 1970) is the unit of analysis. The area within these radii is quantified as to the kinds and densities of economic plants available, numbers of plant communities and areas thereof to identify ecotonal situations, kinds of lithic resources available, kinds of physiographic zones and areas thereof, estimated amount of water available, estimated kinds, amounts and seasonal patterns of game. The various site subsets can be compared to each other, to the population as a whole and to a randomly generated series of hypothetical site locations to elucidate the variables and combinations thereof. Chi-square in its several applications will provide a suitable test of significance.

The four levels of analysis outlined above constitute the basic examination of the data that will be required to elucidate the patterns of site location for management purposes. Beyond the guidelines above, there are many other ways of looking at the data. Which particular methods will be suitable depends on the quality of the data. Further, methods of site location and site catchment analysis are rapidly expanding in archaeology. Green's application of percentage difference and comparison of means plus stepwise multiple regression to analysis of locations of prehistoric Mayan sites in northern British Honduras is one example of methods applicable to inventory data (Green 1973). Site location models can be generated from our current understanding of past economic behavior using mini-max theory and other useful modeling techniques, for comparison against site locational data. While outcomes of these approaches cannot be specified at this time, in similar work they are proving to be sensitive, insightful techniques for examining patterns of site location and identifying the factors that are the most significant determinants of site locations, and thus will be the most accurate predictors for management studies.

POTENTIAL INVENTORY AREAS

From an archaeological viewpoint, the California Desert does not emerge as including some areas of extremely high priority for archaeology contrasting with other, very low, priority areas. Rather than regionally based priorities, the following considerations are important in selecting archaeological inventory areas in the California Desert.

1. The need to identify and protect areas where the archaeological resources remain relatively undamaged.

2. The need to inventory and protect or recover the remaining archaeological values in areas receiving heavy damage.

3. Current research trends dictate some priorities:

    a. the extent of prehistoric and early historic agriculture among the California Indians has created interest in such diverse areas as the Imperial-Coachella Valleys, Lake Mojave and the Eureka Valley.

    b. continuing importance of the California Desert in research into earlier periods of man's occupance of the New World focusing interest on areas of the desert where relict features of Late Pleistocene environments are evident such as the Mojave sink and the Pluvial Pinto River drainage through Palen and Ford Lakes.

4. If predictive patterns are to emerge from the archaeological inventory that will have desert-wide utility, the distribution of the inventory areas will be crucial. Adequate geographic dispersion throughout the area, inclusion of upland areas, closed basins, and through-flowing drainages will be important. Adequate dispersal among the territories assigned to the ethnographic peoples of the California Desert will be another way of checking the distribution.

With the above guidelines in mind, and recognizing that priorities will change due to changes in use pattern and impact on the California Desert, and also with changing research interests in the desert, the following areas are recommended as inventory areas, in addition to the Yuha and El Paso/Red Mountain areas already designated by the BLM.

New York and Providence Mountain Area, Including the Clark Mountains

The area is of considerable archaeological interest in that it presents a very full range of desert vegetation and environments, from extensive areas of pinyon-juniper to the creosote bush communities. Preliminary work in the area by the San Bernardino County Museum and Emma Lou Davis indicate it is rich in archaeological resources. While not heavily impacted at present, the area has been opened to access by a BLM road and campsites, and impact is expected to increase.

Saline-Eureka Valleys

These valleys are reported to contain a great wealth of archaeological remains, spanning at least the past 3,500 years (Robarchek, "A Survey of Archaeological Resources in the Saline-Eureka Valley Area," for BLM) and are suffering much illicit collecting and excavation. The area would provide a sample of archaeology pertinent to the Great Basin Shoshoneans who occupied the northern part of the California Desert. Recent examination of the Eureka Valley indicates that the remains of a late prehistoric irrigation system may be discerned there, suggesting for the first time that some aboriginal agriculture may have been practiced there.

Chuckwalla Valley, Including Palen and Ford Dry Lakes and the McCoy Mountains

In Pluvial times this valley was the seat of a major drainage from Pinto Wash which probably emptied into the Colorado River. It has a high research value in offering the opportunity to gain a fresh, modern perspective on the classic Pinto complex dating 1,000-3,000 BC defined in the 1930's in Pinto Basin. The area includes evidence of trails and sleeping circles of considerable antiquity and appears to be an excellent area for studying the long term changes in late Pleistocene-Holocene climatic change and man's adaptation to it. In more recent times the Yuma-Mojave trail passed through it and it was a contact zone between the Coachella Valley and the Colorado River peoples.

The area is receiving medium impact at present with mining having caused much past damage. Anticipated opening of the area by the BLM will increase the impact to serious levels, since much of the archaeology is on the surface and is extremely vulnerable.

Chemehuevi Valley, Including the Turtle and Whipple Mountains

This area contains archaeological resources that have received limited impact so far except for World War II military damage. It offers the opportunity to study the prehistory of some of the Colorado River agricultural peoples and the nature of their floodplain cultivation. The Turtle Mountains are thought to have had a permanent village and to represent the opportunity to study a contrasting, non-riverine adaptation within this inventory area.

Picacho Mountains, Including the Area South and East of the Chocolate Mountains to the Colorado River and the Mexican Border

Although little work has been done in this area, indications are that it has a high level of archaeological resources, including an extremely important, extensive archaeological zone in the Picachos. Work by Malcolm Rogers indicates that evidence for human occupation spans many thousand years. The area includes rock alignments, trails, cleared house rings and cairns. The Picacho Mountains have suffered low impact so far except for mining. Other areas have experienced heavy impact due to the military. Geothermal explorations and development may pose an additional threat to the area.

Mojave Sink, Including Cave Canyon, the Mouth of the Mojave River and Associated Dune Fields and the Area of Pleistocene Lake Mojave

This is the area where the classic Lake Mojave complex was defined, and the relationship of man to the now extinct lake of 9,000-10,000 years ago remains under investigation. Situated on the major interior drainage in the California Desert, it has long been a focus of human habitation. Recently the possibility of aboriginal agriculture has been raised for the Mojave sink. The area is cut by a major interstate highway and there has been heavy impact on the surface archaeology due to its fragile nature and widespread knowledge of its existence.

San Bernardino Foothills, Along the Northeast Edge of the San Bernardino Mountains

Known occupation of this area dates back to the Sayles Complex which may date about 1,500 BC. In addition to the possibility of finding earlier evidence, the area was intensively occupied in the late period by the Serrano, evidenced by village sites along the skirt of the hills and special activity sites such as roasting pits farther up the drainages. Trade routes from the Mojave into the Morongo River valley passed through here. The area continues to suffer major impacts from small tract subdivision, pothunting and con-struction of transmission lines to feed the Los Angeles metropolitan area.

In addition to the priority areas listed above, the following areas would also be useful inventory areas:

1. Amargosa River drainage

2. A transect area from the Santa Rosa Mountains across the Coachella Valley to the Orocopia Mountains

3. Calico Mountain area including Black Mountain, Alvord Mountains, Lone Mountain, Superior Lake and Murphy Wells

4. Area including Bristol, Cadiz and Dale dry lakes

5. Old Woman Mountain area

6. Panamint Valley

SCHEDULING

It is recommended that the archaeological inventory be executed in a five year period, with an initial sample of 3-4 inventory areas studied during the first two years and the remainder studied in the third and fourth years with the fifth year to complete analysis and reports.

Year
1. Selection of 3-4 inventory areas for archaeological resource analysis. Initiation of first stage sampling in these areas, with on-line monitoring and data synthesis. Initiation of the ethnographic-ethnohistoric component.

2. Second stage sample designed and executed with on-line monitoring and data synthesis. Re-examination of sampling design and procedures, and incorporation of needed changes. Completion of ethnographic-ethnohistoric component.

3. Analysis and report of results of archaeological resource study completion for first set of areas. First stage sampling in remaining areas initiated, with on-line monitoring and analysis.

4. Second stage sampling in remaining areas with on-line monitoring and analysis.

5. Completion of analysis of data, report preparation and management recommendations.

Initiation of the archaeological inventory in any inventory area should be placed so that initial mapping of vegetation communities, water resources and physiography by other elements are available at the beginning of the archaeological work to provide for stratification of the area for sampling.

LITERATURE CITED

Bettinger, Robert and R. E. Taylor
    1973   Suggested Revisions in Interior Southern California Archaeological
           Sequences. In press.

Bettinger, Robert
    1973   Personal communication.

Green, Ernestene
    1973   Location Analysis of Prehistoric Maya Sites in Northern British
           Honduras, _American Antiquity_, vol. 38, no. 3, pp. 279-293.

Jarman, M. R.
    1972   A Territorial Model for Archaeology: A Behavioral and Geographical
           Approach. In _Models in Archaeology_, ed. by David L. Clark, pp.
           705-734.

Kish, Leslie
    1965   _Survey Sampling_. John Wiley and Sons, New York.

Plog, Fred and James N. Hill
    1971   Explaining Variability in the Distribution of Sites. In _The
           Distribution of Prehistoric Population Aggregates_, ed. by George
           J. Gummerman. Prescott College Anthropological Reports, No. 1,
           pp. 7-36.

Siegel, Sidney
    1956   _Nonparametric Statistics for the Behavioral Sciences_. McGraw-Hill
           Book Co.

Thomas, David H.
    1969   Regional Sampling in Archaeology: A Pilot Great Basin Research
           Design. _Annual Report_, UCLA Archaeological Survey, vol. 11, pp.
           89-100.

Vita-Finzi, C. and E. S. Higgs
    1970   Prehistoric Economy in the Mount Carmel Area of Palestine: Site
           Catchment Analysis. _Proceedings of the Prehistoric Society_, vol.
           36, pp. 1-37.

ACKNOWLEDGEMENTS

The Archaeological Inventory of the California Desert: A Proposed
Methodology as assembled by Dr. Margaret L. Weide for the Archaeological
Research Unit of the University of California, Riverside, with the cooperation
of the California Desert Archaeological Committee of the Society for California
Archaeology. Dr. Lowell Bean, California State University, Hayward, contributed
toward the ethnographic-ethnohistoric component. The cooperation and interest
of the Riverside District and Desert Planning staffs of the Bureau of Land
Management is gratefully acknowledged, particularly Herrick Hanks, Wesley
Chambers and James Hagihara. The comments of Dr. James Hill, Dr. Sylvia
Broadbent, Robert Bettinger, Philip Wilke and Roberta Greenwood are especially
acknowledged, as are the many other archaeologists who contributed their
comments and ideas.

The Archaeological Inventory of the California Desert: A Proposed
Methodology as presented here was designed to articulate closely with the
inventory plans of the California Desert Study as they stood in the fall of
1973, and may require modification as those plans evolve.